WOMEN TRAILBREAKERS

An Inspirational and Guided Journal for Girls to Connect with Courageous Women so as to Find Their Own Trailblazing Traits

Sarah Moukhliss, Ed.S.

Women Trailbreakers: An Inspirational and Guided Journal For Girls to Connect with Courageous Women so as to Find Their Own Trailblazing Traits

Copyright © 2020 by Sarah Moukhliss

All rights reserved. No part of this book may be reproduced or used in any manner without written permission of the copyright owner except for the use of quotations in a book review. For more information, email madi@BigLittlePress.com.

First Edition: October 2020
Book design by Project 100
Book Cover design by Michelle Gruyé-Hallam
Artwork created digitally using Clip Studio Paint
Text Type: Short Stack, Long Loving Letters, and Orange Juice

ISBN 978-1-7333217-4-7 (paperback)

www.BigLittlePress.com

DEDICATION

This book is dedicated to my two beautiful, trailbreaking daughters, Nora & Salma, and to all the girls and young women who dream of big things.

DEFINITION OF TRAILBREAKER

1. A leader or pioneer in a particular field
2. A person who blazes a trail

NOTE TO GIRLS

Dear Gutsy Girl Reader and Writer,

A trailbreaker is a pioneer or leader in a particular field or profession. A trailbreaker sounds a lot like the word "trailblazer." Both are important words for you to remember and are almost interchangeable! I sat with both words for a while before I settled on using trailbreaker for this journal's title. The women within these pages were not only good at what they did, but they were also fearless. They metaphorically took a shovel to dig out new paths for other girls to follow.

A trailbreaker is not just someone who lived long ago. She can live today. She may be your teacher, mother, or neighbor. She may or may not be famous nor easy to find in a history book. This journal presents trailbreaking women in chronological order. Therefore, the first woman lived the longest ago, and the last entry is still a girl like you!

A trailbreaker can even be found within YOU. This journal will encourage YOU to think and act like a trailbreaker. Although these women are very different, they have similarities too. I hope you can make the connections from one woman to the next and continue to make connections back to yourself.
The last couple pages are kept blank so that you can add your own trailbreaker role models. It is impossible to gather every smart, important woman for one journal, but it is important that YOUR favorite trailbreaker be a part of your writing journey.

Go get them, and happy journaling!

FATIMA AL-FIHRI
(CIRCA 9TH CENTURY)

Fatima lived long ago in the 800's A.D. After moving from Tunisia to Morocco, she decided to create something--the first of its kind! She established the world's first degree-granting university.

Thanks to Fatima, people all over the world can attend colleges and universities to receive degrees such as the bachelor's degrees, master's degrees, and doctoral degrees!

Trailbreakers Value Lifelong Learning

Trailbreakers believe in lifelong learning. Being curious and stretching oneself mentally is important for self-growth. It is never too early to think about your future.

What do you want to become when you grow up?
Explore:

https://www.bls.gov/kas.students/careers/career-exploration.htm.

_____

_____

_____

_____

_____

Research Your Dream Job

Research your dream job and what degree is required.

My dream job:

_____

_____

_____

College degree needed:

_____

_____

_____

_____

WILLIAMINA FLEMING
(1857-1911)

Williamina was once a maid until her boss, a Harvard University astronomer, invited her to study the stars. She proved to be an exceptional astronomer's assistant. Williamina spent her career helping to develop a star classification system based on a star's light spectra. She organized thousands of stars into their appropriate categories. She also discovered hundreds of variable stars and identified what we now know to be the white dwarf.

Trailbreakers Take Risks!

Williamina was courageous to give astronomy a try. She could have played it safe and remained a maid, but she did not. She took a risk and tried something new and outside of her comfort zone. **Think** about something that you are good at. Now, think about something that you would love to try, but you have little-to-no experience with it.

I am good at:

_____

But....

I would love to try:

_____

_____

Write an Acrostic Poem!

It takes courage to take a risk. Celebrate courage with acrostic poetry. An acrostic poem is formed by spelling out an important word. For each letter of the important word, think of a new word that describes the important word. Help complete the poem.

C onfidence

O

U

R

A

G

E

GERTRUDE BENHAM
(1867-1938)

Gertrude was an adventurer, explorer, and a mountaineer. She did many cool things such as circumnavigating the world multiple times. She climbed hundreds of mountain peaks. In fact, in 1909, Gertrude became the first European explorer to climb Mount Kilimanjaro. She did this alone as her guide left her mid-journey.

Trailbreakers Don't Need an Audience

Stop and think: How would you feel if you accomplished a goal, but there was no one around to watch?

_____

_____

_____

_____

_____

_____

_____

_____

_____

_____

Reflection Time

Trailbreakers seem to maintain a lot of intrinsic motivation. Intrinsic motivation is the behaviors that drive people to do better because of how it makes them feel inside.

What activity makes you happy?

_____

_____

_____

_____

_____

_____

Compete Against Yourself

What activity or hobby do you want to perfect? How will you reach this goal?

I want to get better at:

_____

_____

I will reach my goal by:

_____

_____

_____

_____

My Notes

MIGNON TALBOT
(1869-1950)

Mignon was an American-born paleontologist who became the first woman to discover and name a dinosaur. The Podokesaurus Holyokensis (POH-doh-kuh-SAWR-us HOL-ee-o-KEN-sis) is a petite, chicken-sized, meat-eating dinosaur. She published about her discovery in 1911.

Trailbreakers Create Ripple Effects Across Other Fields

There is an art form called paleoart. Paleoartists pay close attention to what paleontologists discover. They examine the bones and create an image of what the dinosaur may have looked like.

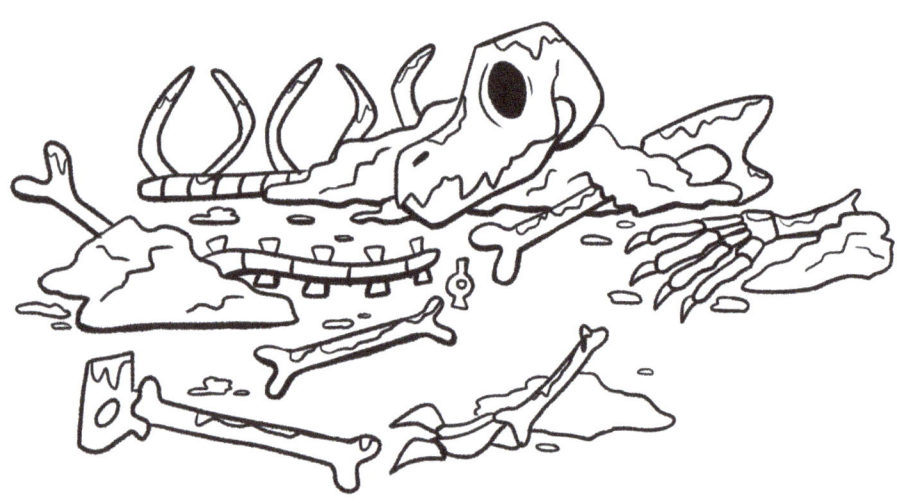

Practice Paleoart

After looking at the dinosaur bones on the previous page, draw a picture here of what that dinosaur looked like:

MARIAN ANDERSON
(1897-1993)

Marian was a talented opera singer who lived during a time when people judged her by the color of her skin. Despite obstacles, she sang with the famous Metropolitan Opera. In 1939, she was invited to sing at the Constitution Hall in Washington, D.C. However, it was canceled because some people refused to allow her to use the space. Instead of giving up, she changed the venue to an outdoor space at the Lincoln Memorial where a whopping 75,000 people attended to hear her sing!

Trailbreakers Take Lemons and Make Lemonade

Have you ever heard of the saying "when life gives you lemons, you make lemonade"? Trailbreakers do not give up. When something goes wrong, Trailbreakers work with the situation to find something better. Marian did not quit after hearing that her show in the performance hall was canceled. Instead, she moved her performance outside and got to perform for 75,000 admirers!

Reflect

Think of a time when you took a lemon moment and chose to make lemonade.

My lemon moment was:

_____
_____
_____
_____

I turned a negative situation around and made lemonade by:

_____
_____
_____
_____
_____

How to Make Lemonade out of a Lemon Situation

First, I.....
_____
_____

Then, I ....
_____
_____

Next, I.......
_____
_____

Finally, I....
_____
_____

How to Make Lemonade

Ingredients:
2 cups water
1 cup sugar
1 cup lemon juice (4 lemons)

AMELIA EARHART
(1897-1937)

Amelia Earhart was a famous aviator who became the first female pilot to fly across the Atlantic Ocean. Because few women were pilots during her time, she developed a club to encourage other women to fly!

Trailbreakers Know That There Is Strength in Numbers

Trailbreakers tend not to want to keep their passions to themselves. They want to share their knowledge and love for something with others. They encourage others to follow in their footsteps. Think of an activity that you LOVE to do! Research to see if there are any local clubs to join.

Find a Club

Club name:

_____

Contact information:

_____
_____
_____

Why is it beneficial to share an activity or hobby that you love with others?

_____
_____
_____
_____
_____
_____
_____
_____

FRIDA KAHLO
(1907-1954)

Frida Kahlo, a famous artist, originally wanted to become a doctor when she grew up. However, a bad accident left her unable to go to medical school. Having to choose a new path, she taught herself to paint. Her paintings are famous as they include many symbols and colorful images from her Mexican heritage. Today, you can find Frida's artwork exhibited in famous museums throughout the world.

Trailbreakers Are Flexible

It would have been easy for Frida to give up and feel bad about herself when she was unable to fulfill her first dream. Instead, she redirected her energies to art and developed a special style all on her own.

Reflect

Think about your life as a series of paths which lead you in different directions. These different paths represent your different interests and hobbies.

What are your favorite interests and hobbies?

_____

_____

_____

Your Self-Portrait

Frida is famous for her self-portraits. She had a special style. Using your own artistic style, create your own self-portrait:

My Notes

INGEBORG SYLLM-RAPOPORT
(1912–2017)

Ingeborg was a German Holocaust survivor who was unable to defend her doctoral dissertation in 1938 because of religious discrimination. At age 102, she defended her thesis and passed! Despite the 77 years in between the time she should have defended, she finished the process to honor all victims of the Holocaust.

Trailbreakers Are Patient

Ingeborg was very patient. She waited 77 years to become Dr. Syllm-Rapoport. Good things are worth waiting for.

What in your life requires patience?

Concrete Poetry

Use the clock picture below as a template for your concrete poetry. Describe patience. Your words should wrap around the clock--making a circle. When your words take on the shape of what you write about, it becomes a concrete poem.

KATHERINE JOHNSON
(1918-2020)

Katherine worked with NASA scientists and calculated a trajectory path for Apollo 11 to land on the Moon. Johnson had to defy racial and gender barriers to work at NASA as very few were women or African American.

Trailbreakers Open Doors For Others

Because of Katherine's bravery, brains, and success, she inspired other women and African Americans to apply for jobs at NASA.

Color in the picture.

Girls in STEM

With a parent's permission, Google "Girls in STEM." Find the three most interesting websites about girls and young women growing up to work in science, technology, engineering, or math fields.

Write the 3 websites down to visit and learn about later:

1. _____

2. _____

3. _____

MARIA TALLCHIEF
(1925-2013)

Maria always loved to dance. Maria tried ballet. She excelled at it and decided to move to New York City at age 17 to find dancing roles. Maria was rejected during her auditions because of her Native American heritage. People had a hard time believing that a Native American could dance classical ballet. Other dancers suggested that she change her last name as it did not sound like the name of a ballerina. Maria ignored these comments and kept her name.

Despite numerous rejections, Tallchief continued to audition and eventually landed the prima ballerina role with the New York City Ballet. Maria pushed through rejection and broke barriers for other Native American girls who dreamed to dance with ballet companies.

Trailbreakers Do Not Take Rejections Too Personally

Trailbreakers are good at losing. They find the opportunity to reflect on the loss and then get back up and try again. For as many ballet companies that fell in love with Maria's talents there were just as many that did not invite her to dance with their ballerinas.

Stop and Think

How do you feel when you lose? Perhaps you came in last at a talent competition or you failed to win a game of checkers or chess.

_____
_____
_____
_____

How could you use that failure to grow as a person?

_____
_____
_____
_____
_____
_____
_____
_____

CORETTA SCOTT KING
(1927–2006)

Coretta, a mother, musician, and civil rights activist, was married to the very famous Dr. Martin Luther King Jr., a civil rights activist. Coretta believed in her husband and supported his dream of equality and peace. Right after her husband's untimely death, she marched to support a labor strike to continue Dr. King's dream. Throughout the remainder of her years, she raised her children and traveled the world to speak about the dangers of racism. The Coretta Scott King Book Award is a prestigious, children's book award named in her honor.

Trailbreakers Persevere

Study the sentences below. When you use one of these sentences during a difficult task or time, you are persevering.

I will keep trying.	I will take a break but try again.	I won't stop.
I won't give up.	I will find those who believe in me.	I won't let others stop me.
I will ask for help.	I will remain positive.	I will believe in myself.

Reflect

Reflect on a time that you persevered through a difficult situation.

SANDRA DAY O'CONNOR
(1930-PRESENT)

Sandra Day O'Connor began her career in law and worked her way up to Associate Justice of the Supreme Court. At the beginning of her career, it was difficult to find a job because most people felt that only men could perform such work. As she moved through her career, she felt a great responsibility to do well so that other women could follow her path.

Trailbreakers Want to Be Good Role Models

Sandra found it important to be a good role model. Stop and think: what makes a good role model?

List Your Role Models

BARBARA HENRY
(1932-PRESENT)

RUBY BRIDGES
(1954-PRESENT)

In 1960, Little Ruby, then student and now activist, entered an all-white school to become the first African American student to attend a traditionally all-white school. The year prior, white students and African American students were required to attend different schools. The day Ruby walked up the steps to her school, many people were excited for change, and other people were angry. Ruby needed to walk with police officers, so she could be safe.

Ms. Henry was Ruby's teacher. Ms. Henry believed that all children deserved to attend school and skin color did not matter. Many of the teachers disagreed with Ms. Henry. Despite this obstacle, Ms. Henry welcomed Ruby into her classroom and taught her the entire school year. Ruby was her only student that year. Ruby and Ms. Henry were brave to stand up for what was right even though so many people disagreed with their points of view.

Trailbreakers Are Brave

Ruby needed a lot of bravery to enter her new school. What does bravery look like? How can you present yourself as being brave?

Take a moment to *list* what bravery looks like. Practice in a mirror. Write down three to four more examples.

1. Head is up

2. Eyes are straight ahead

3. Stand up tall

4. _____

5. _____

6. _____

7. _____

Draw Your Brave Face

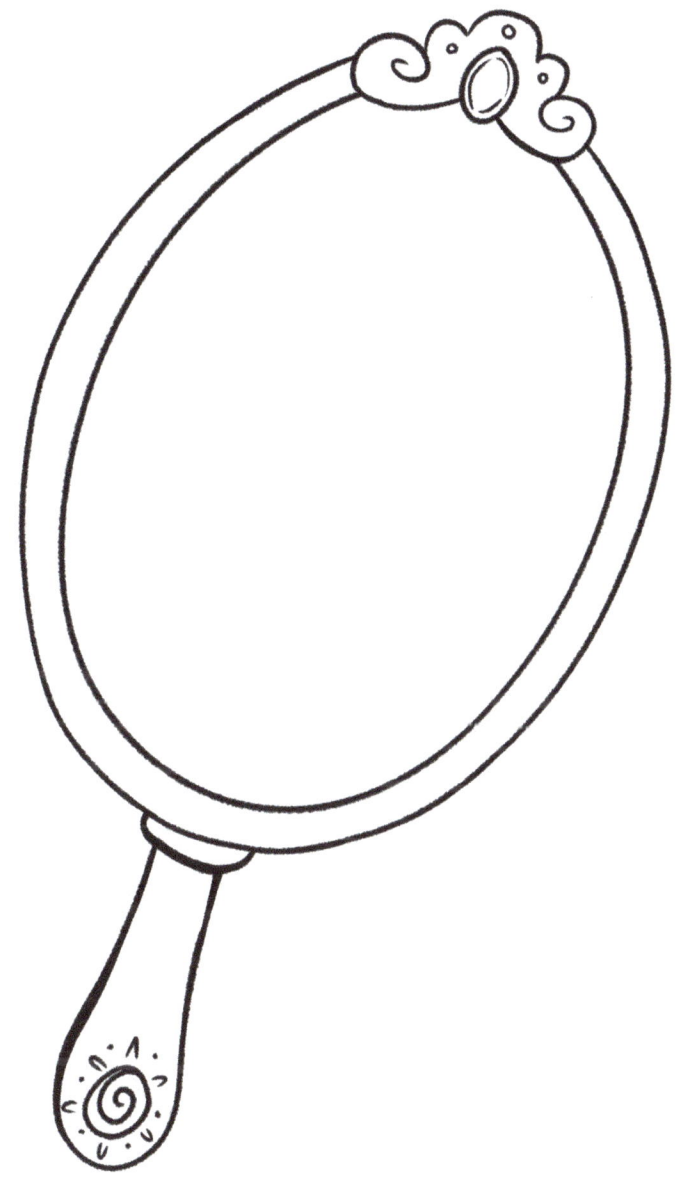

JANE GOODALL
(1934-PRESENT)

Jane, a zoologist, dreamed of working in Africa researching animals. Initially trained as a secretary, she worked with a paleontologist, Louis Leakey, in Africa. Under his guidance and direction, she returned to university to earn a PH.D. in ethology, or animal behavior. Jane Goodall's education is unique as she pursued a PH.D. before earning her undergraduate degree or a master's degree. Jane's research proved that chimpanzees eat more than plants--they also eat meat and insects. Like humans, they can make their own tools.

Trailbreakers Work with Those Who Believe in Them

Jane began her career with no experience with chimpanzees. Although her dream job seemed distant and perhaps impossible for young Jane, those around her saw that she had raw talent. Louis Leaky believed in Jane and encouraged her to obtain a PH.D. about her interests. Trailbreakers surround themselves with people who believe in them.

Make a List

List the people in your life who believe in you:

DOROTHY PITMAN HUGHES
(1938-PRESENT)

GLORIA STEINEM
(1934- PRESENT)

Dorothy Pitman Hughes and Gloria Steinem are successful advocates. Dorothy Pitman Hughes argued for proper childcare, equality for women, and people of color. Gloria argued for women's rights and equality. They teamed up together to use their powers to reach more people-- encouraging as many people as possible to speak up about unfair issues.

Trailbreakers Team Up!

Trailbreakers understand that there is strength in numbers. They often team up with other Trailbreakers.

Who would be on your Trailbreaking Team?

_____
_____
_____
_____

Why?

_____
_____
_____
_____
_____
_____
_____

My Notes

SYLVIA EARLE
(1935-PRESENT)

As a teenager, Sylvia, an oceanographer, tried to develop makeshift scuba gear because she wanted to explore deeper waters. She grew up to become the first woman to explore the ocean's floor. While working on an experiment called the Tektite Project, she led an all-women team to reside in an underwater habitat for two weeks.

Trailbreakers Are Explorers

Trailbreakers explore uncharted territories.

Take the survey. Where would you want to explore?

Rank the order of your interests
(1= Most Interested; 5= Least Interested)

- [ ] The Ocean's Deep
- [ ] A Cave
- [ ] The Solar System
- [ ] The Antarctic
- [ ] Other (fill in the blank)

_____

Design Your Underwater Home

Sylvia designed an underwater habitat for scientists to live in. Draw your underwater home here:

BILLIE JEAN KING
(1943–PRESENT)

Billie Jean is a tennis superstar. She won 39 Grand Slams and 20 championships at Wimbledon. She competed during a time when men did not take women tennis players seriously. This belief bothered Billie Jean. She challenged a male tennis star to a match and beat him. Off the courts, Billie advocated for equal pay for professional women athletes.

Trailbreakers Know What They Are Worth

Brainstorm ways you can earn extra money:

___
___
___
___
___
___

What would you choose to do with your extra money?

___
___
___
___
___
___
___
___

Thinking about Money and Fairness

How would you feel if you were underpaid for your work?

How could you convince others that you deserve more?

DR. BARBARA KLEIN
(1945-PRESENT)

Dr. Barbara Klein is an educator, advocate for gifted children, and a twin psychologist. Barbara was always an inquisitive child. She had a lot of questions about being an identical twin and wondered about what made her different. Her pursuit for individuality ended up becoming her career. Barbara went to college to receive a PH.D. in education and psychology. Today, she works with children and helps parents to understand their unique child. She works with twins so that they better understand how being a twin makes them different than those who are not twins.

Trailbreakers Understand the Importance of Being Themselves

Being yourself is how you set yourself apart from others. Think about how you are unique. You are "you," and there is no one quite like you.

I Am Unique Because...

List all your special qualities that make you unique:

-
-
-
-
-
-
-
-
-
-
-
-
-
-
-
-
-
-

OPRAH WINFREY
(1954-PRESENT)

Oprah, an actress, television personality, and TV producer, grew up very poor. She attended college to become a news anchor and eventually landed her own show, "The Oprah Winfrey Show." After many years of hard work and success, she started the Oprah Magazine and created her own TV network.

Trailbreakers Reinvent Themselves

Trailbreakers are OK with trying new things. Oprah tried to be a TV news anchor and tried making magazines and creating a TV network.

List three new things you would like to try:

1. _____

2. _____

3. _____

Compare and Contrast

Think about what you liked when you were a little girl. Compare that to what you are like now. How are you different? How are you the same? Fill out the Venn Diagram as you brainstorm:

MAE JEMISON
(1956-PRESENT)

Mae, a doctor and astronaut, always loved science--especially astronomy, anthropology, and archaeology! Mae enrolled at Stanford University when she was 16 years old and majored in African American studies and chemical engineering. She forged ahead to receive her doctorate in medicine. Mae was one of a handful of people to be selected into astronaut training and traveled to space in 1992. She has worked as a volunteer for the Peace Corps to help advance the field of medicine in Africa. Today, Mae improves the world by working at her company, Jemison Group, Inc.

Trailbreakers Understand the Sky Is the Limit!

Trailbreakers dream big and then go for it. **Write** down your goals and dreams no matter how impossible they seem to you now.

My goals and dreams:

_____
_____
_____
_____
_____
_____
_____
_____
_____
_____
_____

3, 2, 1, Liftoff!

Color the picture below:

ELLEN DEGENERES
(1958-PRESENT)

Ellen DeGeneres, comedian and actress, has utilized her wit, humor, charm, and authenticity to become a TV sensation. She began her humble career in local stand-up comedy. She was discovered through these performances and landed a role in a TV comedy show. Her fame grew, and she now is the star of the talk show, the *Ellen DeGeneres Show*. Ellen is an advocate for marginalized populations, and her mantra is to be kind to one another.

Trailbreakers Understand the Power of Kindness

Describe a moment when someone was kind toward you. How did that make you feel?

Reflect

What are some ways you can show kindness to others?

MAYA LIN
(1959-PRESENT)

Maya, an architectural designer and artist, designed the Vietnam Veterans Memorial in Washington, D.C. at just 21 years old. She submitted her design to a national design contest and won! Maya went on to design the Civil Rights Memorial and has helped with designing public spaces and libraries.

Trailbreakers Are Creative

Where do your creative powers lie? Are you a:

	Yes	No
Creative storyteller	☐	☐
Creative artist	☐	☐
Creative chef	☐	☐
Creative musician	☐	☐
Creative actor	☐	☐
Creative author	☐	☐

Other:

_____

_____

Creativity is more apt to show up when you suspend what others think of your work, so just go for it and let your creative juices flow!

Get Creative

Take a look at the doodle below and turn it into a fully illustrated masterpiece! What can you create with the first mark?

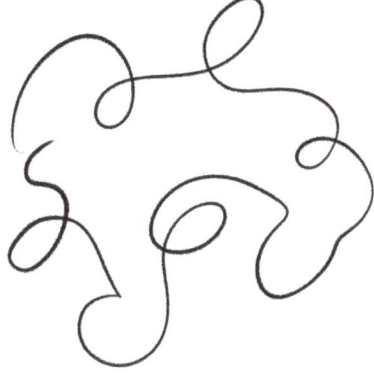

MICHELLE OBAMA
(1964-PRESENT)

Michelle Obama is a lawyer, mother, and wife to former president Barack Obama. She served as First Lady from 2009 to 2017. During her time in the White House, she advocated for healthy foods for children and even planted an organic garden at the White House.

Trailbreakers Work for a Cause!

Michelle believed that healthy food is important for America's children. She turned healthy food accessibility into her cause while she was First Lady. Visit the website:

kidscanmakeadifference.org/what-kids-can-do

Stop and Think

Reflect on a cause that is important to you. **Write** out your strategy on how you can help your cause.

HODA KOTB
(1964-PRESENT)

Hoda has worked as a TV Anchor/TV Personality for NBC and the *Today Show*. Hoda had enjoyed a twenty-year career in journalism before "making it big" to become a nationally-known TV journalist.

Trailbreakers "Keep At It"

Many people may want to become nationally famous for what they do, but trailbreakers know that it may or may not happen, and the most important thing is to keep at what you are passionate about.

What do you love to do?

_____

_____

Can you see yourself doing this in:

	Yes	No
1 year?	☐	☐
5 years?	☐	☐
10 Years?	☐	☐
The rest of your life?	☐	☐

Stop and Think

How may you change as you keep at it?

MIA HAMM
(1972-PRESENT)

Mia is known as one of the best soccer stars in the world. She became well known for her talents in scoring soccer goals at international matches. She is a two-time World Cup winner and an Olympic medalist. Hamm may be best known for growing the popularity of women's soccer throughout the United States. Today, many young girls work hard and hope to follow in her path one day.

Trailbreakers Help to Make It Popular

Before Mia, few American people paid attention to women's soccer as a serious sport. Think of a hobby or activity that you enjoy that others may know little about. How would you persuade them to give it a try?

Here are some examples:

Playing the harmonica
Skipping rope
Collecting rocks

_____
_____
_____
_____
_____
_____
_____

Research

Visit websites to research your under-celebrated activity or hobby. Write down three reasons why this activity is important to you and the world:

1. _____

2. _____

3. _____

DR. JEN WELTER
(1977-PRESENT)

Dr. Jen Welter was the first female to coach an NFL Football team, the Arizona Cardinals, when she landed the role of a coaching intern in 2015. She continued her career to work as a linebacker and special teams' coach for Champion's Indoor Football Texas Revolution. Welter has designed programs for other young women interested in playing and following in her path. Dr. Jen Welter holds a doctoral degree in psychology.

Trailbreakers Break Barriers

Coaching a men's football team was thought to be a man's job until very recently. Because of Dr. Welter, women can now feel more confident in applying for these jobs too.

Have you ever heard someone say:
"That's a boy's game."
"That's a boy's book."
"That's a boy's show."

_____
_____
_____
_____
_____
_____
_____

Reflection Time

Is there such a thing as a boy's game or a girl's game? Why or why not?

JILLIAN MERCADO
(1987–PRESENT)

Jillian is a successful model, actress, and activist. She is a graduate of the Fashion Institute of Technology. Jillian lives with a condition called muscular dystrophy and uses an electric wheelchair to get around. Initially, she hoped to work for a fashion magazine so she could scout out models with disabilities. It soon became apparent that she could either be the scout looking for models or the actual model. Jillian chose modeling and has graced many runways. Jillian uses her platform to speak up for others with disabilities and to ensure that all runways have wheelchair accessibility for models and those watching.

Trailbreakers Do Not Let Their Physical Limitations Stop Them!

We all have physical limitations. Some may be more obvious than others. Perhaps you have a hard time touching your toes. Because of this fact, you shy away from trying out those relaxing yoga stretches and poses.

Never let what your body cannot do stop you from trying new things.

Reflect

As I think about my body and my body's limitations, just because I can't do _____,

won't stop me from trying _____.

YUJA WANG
(1987-PRESENT)

Yuja is a prodigy pianist who studied music at Central Conservatory of Music in Beijing, China, and at the Curtis Institute of Music in Philadelphia. By the age of 21, she was known worldwide for her talents and her fashionable performance-wear. Yuja forgoes traditional long black dresses for bright, flashy, glittery ones. Her choice to go against the grain in what a classical pianist should wear for a classical performance along with her talents have sparked conversations from people of all ages. Yuja brings the hip and cool component into the world of classical music.

Trailbreakers Bring Their Own Style to Their Practice

Describe your style:

Rock out Your Style

Draw a picture of you rocking your most favorite style:

EMMA WATSON
(1990-PRESENT)

Emma is an actress and a feminist. She has dabbled in modeling too. Emma is best known for her role as Hermione Granger in the *Harry Potter* movies. She landed the role as Hermione with no former acting experiences. Like Hermione, Emma values intelligence. Despite a hectic schedule, she attended Brown University and majored in English.

Trailbreakers Know That It Is Beautiful to Be Brainy

What brain-growing activities do you enjoy?

☐ Chess

☐ Rubik's Cube

☐ Riddles

☐ Puzzles

☐ Science Experiments

☐ Crossword Puzzles

☐ Other _____

My Notes

SIMONE BILES
(1997-PRESENT)

Simone, an American gymnast, is the most decorated gymnast in the history of gymnastics. She has won a lot of medals! Simone's performances are so advanced that there are movements named in her honor. Her triple double move is a combination of two backflips with three twists.

Trailbreakers Are Fearless!

Fearlessness involves believing in oneself. List people you know who are fearless. They can be people in your real life, people you have seen on TV, or characters from stories or movies.

Make a list of your fearless role models. List one trait that helps them overcome their fears.

Name	Trait

List Your Fearless Traits

1. _____

2. _____

3. _____

4. _____

5. _____

6. _____

7. _____

ISABELLA SPRINGMUHL TEJADA
(1997-PRESENT)

Isabella is a Guatemalan fashion designer. Isabella started a company called Down to Xjabelle, a clothing line that weaves Guatemalan culture with inclusive clothing designs. Born with Down syndrome, Isabella Springmuhl Tejada understood firsthand how difficult it was to find clothes that fit her proportionately and set out to make a company that sells flattering clothes for everyone--including those with disabilities. Having initially been rejected to attend her dream colleges, she persisted and enrolled in online design classes. She has showcased her designs at London's Fashion Week and other international venues.

Trailbreakers Notice a Problem and Work to Solve It

Use the mind map and write down a problem that you would like to solve in the center circle. Your problem can be as big or as small as you want. In the outside circles, brainstorm different solutions to your problem.

My Notes

MALALA YOUSAFZAI
(1997-PRESENT)

Malala campaigns for girls and education. As a student in Pakistan, Malala spoke up about her opinion on the importance of an education for girls by making a blog. Some people did not like her opinions and shot her. Malala survived, moved to England for treatment, healed, and continues to speak out about girl's rights and education. In 2015, Malala opened a school for Syrian refugees in Lebanon. She became the United Nation's youngest UN Messenger of Peace.

Trailbreakers Refuse to Be Bullied

Stop and think: have you ever been bullied?

If so, how did that make you feel?

Brainstorm

How can you stop bullying in your school or your community?

Billie Eilish
(2001-present)

Billie is a singer and a songwriter. Despite her young age, she has won multiple Grammy awards for her work. She is well known for her unique singing style as well as her sense of fashion. Eilish wants her fans to focus on her music and not her wardrobe. Therefore, she chooses to dress in understated, baggy clothing. Billie is open about having Tourette syndrome, a condition that causes involuntary sounds and movements.

Trailbreakers Do Not Let Others Define Them

My most favorite music is:

_____

_____

The outfit that makes me feel most like me is:

_____

_____

My most favorite way I wear my hair is:

_____

_____

_____

_____

Define Yourself

You are asked to write about yourself so that you can be added to a Dictionary of Important Women. **Write** 3-5 sentences about yourself:

GRETA THUNBERG
(2003-PRESENT)

Greta is one of the youngest climate change activists speaking up and making an impact. Greta skipped school to host a strike outside of Sweden's congressional buildings. She speaks at rallies and even spoke up at the United Nations Climate Change Summit to urge others to protect the environment. Adults have coined this movement the "Greta Effect." Greta is proof that you are never too young to make a difference.

Trailbreakers Speak Passionately about What They Believe in

Greta loves the environment. What are you passionate about? What would you do to protect what you love?

My Notes

Now, it is time to **add** a trailbreaker that you love to your journal...

My Trailbreaker

Name: _____

Reasons Why I Love My Trailbreaker

My Trailbreaker

Name: _____

Reasons Why I Love My Trailbreaker

I Am a Trailbreaker

My Trailbreaker Traits

REFERENCES

Fatima Al-Fihri (Circa 9th Century)
https://manchesteruniversitypress.co.uk/articles/fatima-al-fihri-founder-worlds-first-university/
https://selfrescuingprincesssociety.tumblr.com/post/66911683868/historicwomen-fatima-al-fihri-880-fatima

Williamina Fleming (1857-1911)
Kilzer, N. V. (2020). Fleming, Williamina. In World Book Advanced. Retrieved from
https://worldbookonline.com/advanced/article?id=ar756775

Gertrude Benham (1867-1938)
https://www.bustle.com/p/11-overlooked-women-from-history-according-to-10-female-historians-15961727

Mignon Talbot (1869-1950)
Stricker, Beth. (2017). Daring to dig: Adventures of women in American paleontology. Paleontological Research Institution.
https://www.wonderopolis.org/wonders?tag=paleoart

Marian Anderson (1897-1993)
Anderson, Marian. (2020). In World Book Kids. Retrieved from https://www.worldbookonline.com/kids/home#article/ar830060

Amelia Earhart (1897-1937)
Bednarek, J.R. (2020). Earhart, Amelia. In World Book Student. Retrieved from
https://worldbookonline.com/student-new/#/article/home/ar171340/earhart

Frida Kahlo (1907-1954)
Leveton, D. (2020). Kahlo, Frida. In World Book Student. Retrieved from

https://www.worldbookonline.com/student-new/#/article/home/ar293750/Frida%20Kahlo

Ingeborg Syllm-Rapoport (1912-2017)
https://www.jpost.com/Diaspora/Woman-102-receives-PhD-denied-to-her-by-Nazis-in-1938-405582

Katherine Johnson (1918-2020)
González, E.E. (2020). Johnson, Katherine Goble. In World Book Student. Retrieved from
https://www.worldbookonline.com/student-new/#/article/home/ar757732/katherine%20johnson

Maria Tallchief (1925-2013)
https://www.womenshistory.org/education-resources/biographies/maria-tallchief

Coretta Scott King (1927-2006)
Garrow, D. J. (2020). King, Coretta Scott. In World Book Advanced. Retrieved from
https://worldbookonline.com/advanced/article?id=ar300318
https://www.womenshistory.org/education-resources/biographies/coretta-scott-king

Sandra Day O'Connor (1930-Present)
Hutchinson, D.J. (2020). O'Connor, Sandra Day. In World Book Student. Retrieved from
https://worldbookonline.com/student-new/#/article/home/ar399040/o'connor

Barbara Henry (1932- Present), Teacher & Ruby Bridges (1954-Present), Former Student and Civil Rights Activist.
https://www.bostonglobe.com/magazine/2014/06/27/teaching-ruby-bridges-reflecting-classroom-that-made-civil-rights-history/r0ozyM4GQWzD25g5mzhtqN/story.html

Jane Goodall (1934-Present)
https://www.biography.com/scientist/jane-goodall

Gloria Steinem (1934- Present) and Dorothy Pitman Hughes (1938-Present)
Epstein, C.F. (2020). Steinem, Gloria. In World Book Student. Retrieved from
https://worldbookonline.com/student-new/#/article/home/ar531845/steinem
https://en.wikipedia.org/wiki/Dorothy_Pitman_Hughes

Sylvia Earle (1935-Present)
https://www.parley.tv/updates/2017/3/7/five-pioneers-of-ocean-exploration-who-happen-to-be-women
https://www.britannica.com/biography/Sylvia-Earle

Billie Jean King (1943-Present)
Lance, T. (2020). King, Billie Jean. In World Book Student. Retrieved from
https://www.worldbookonline.com/student-new/#/article/home/ar300316/billie%20jean%20king

Dr. Barbara Klein (1945-Present)
http://drbarbaraklein.squarespace.com/

Oprah Winfrey (1954-Present)
Feder, R. (2020). Winfrey, Oprah. In World Book Student. Retrieved from
https://worldbookonline.com/student-new/#/article/home/ar606350/oprah%20winfrey

Mae Jemison (1956-Present)
Kozloski, L.D. (2020). Jemison, Mae Carol. In World Book Student. Retrieved from
https://www.worldbookonline.com/student-new/#/article/home/ar287210

https://starchild.gsfc.nasa.gov/docs/StarChild/whos_who_level2/jemison.html

Ellen DeGeneres (1958-Present)
DeGeneres, Ellen. (2020). In World Book Student. Retrieved from https://worldbookonline.com/student-new/#/article/home/ar754289/ellen%20degeneres

Maya Lin (1959- Present)
Adams, N. (2020). Lin, Maya. In World Book Student. Retrieved from https://worldbookonline.com/student-new/#/article/home/ar755658/Maya%20Lin

Michelle Obama (1964- Present)
Mieczkowski, Y. (2020). Obama, Michelle Robinson. In World Book Student. Retrieved from https://www.worldbookonline.com/student-new/#/article/home/ar753570/michelle%20obama
https://obamawhitehouse.archives.gov/administration/first-lady-michelle-obama

Hoda Kotb (1964- Present)
https://www.biography.com/media-figure/hoda-kotb

Mia Hamm (1972-Present)
Milbert, N. (2020). Hamm, Mia. In World Book Student. Retrieved from https://worldbookonline.com/student-new/#/article/home/ar751566/mia%20hamm

Dr. Jen Welter (1977- Present)
https://www.jenwelter.com/keynote

Jillian Mercado (1987-Present)
https://www.huffpost.com/entry/jillian-mercado-disabled-latina-model_n_5d5aa4b1e4b0eb875f26d49d

Yuja Wang (1987- Present)
http://yujawang.com/about/

Emma Watson (1990-Present)
https://www.biography.com/actor/emma-watson

Simone Biles (1997-Present)
https://www.cbssports.com/general/news/simone-biles-has-two-new-signature-moves-that-will-be-named-after-her-following-world-championships-performance/

Normile, D. (2020). Biles, Simone. In World Book Student. Retrieved from https://www.worldbookonline.com/student-new/#/article/home/ar757047/simone%20biles

Isabella Springmuhl Tejada (1997-Present)
https://listverse.com/2019/12/03/10-of-the-most-successful-people-with-down-syndrome/

Malala Yousafzai (1997-Present)
Jalal, A. (2020). Yousafzai, Malala. In World Book Student. Retrieved from https://www.worldbookonline.com/student-new/#/article/home/ar755365/malala

Billie Eilish (2001-Present)
Guibert, G. (2020). Eilish, Billie. In World Book Student. Retrieved from https://www.worldbookonline.com/student-new/#/article/home/ar758388/billie%20eilish

Greta Thunberg (2003-Present)
https://time.com/person-of-the-year-2019-greta-thunberg/

COOL RESOURCES TO EXPLORE

A Mighty Girl
https://www.amightygirl.com/

Girls Can Crate
https://www.girlscancrate.com/

Girls Going Global
http://www.girlsgoingglobal.org/

Girls in the Game
https://www.girlsinthegame.org/

Girls on the Run
https://www.girlsontherun.org/

Girls Rock Camp Foundation
http://www.girlsrockcampfoundation.org/

Girls STEAM Institute
https://girlsteaminstitute.org/

Kazoo
https://www.kazoomagazine.com/

ABOUT THE AUTHOR

Sarah Moukhliss is a mother, teacher, and librarian. She feels that it is important for girls to see their current and evolving selves when reading about great women Trailbreakers. Moukhliss lives in Florida with her husband, two daughters, several finches, and a dog.

ABOUT THE ILLUSTRATOR

Marie Delon is a Mexican illustrator based in the city of Puebla, Mexico. Her work includes mostly digital techniques and mixed media. In the past, she has worked for independent publications, videogames and zines, children books and advertising, both national and international. Marie is a full-time graphic designer and implements her illustrations in her daily job.

www.ingramcontent.com/pod-product-compliance
Lightning Source LLC
Chambersburg PA
CBHW040510110526
44587CB00045B/4191